PLEASE DON'T HUG ME

Written by Cathy Acampora

Produced by Plymouth County 4-H Extension

44 Obery St., Plymouth, MA 02360

774-404-7020

For more information on the 4-H program contact Plymouth County 4-H or visit the webpage

www.plymouthcounty4h.org

"Simple steps on how to live safely with dogs is beautifully depicted in Please Don't Hug Me: a guide to dog safety and being a good dog friend. Stunning photographs of dogs in real-life situations are accompanied with clear do's and don't's that can be understood by children of any age and adults too. Please Don't Hug Me is a must read for every child so they can have a positive relationship with dogs throughout their life. As a former librarian, every public and school library needs to own this book and put it on their summer reading list and every Therapy Dog handler needs to own a copy and use it as a resource on their visits." - Patti, Brookfield CT

"Packed with valuable information to keep kids safe, Please Don't Hug Me is a kid friendly, relatable book adults everywhere should share with the children they love. I own a copy and so should you."- Nancy, Lake Lure NC

"It's simple, it entertains and it's on point. This book is a gift , not only to the children it's teaching, but dog owners everywhere. As every child becomes more knowledgeable about the do's and don't's around dogs, all parents, dog owners and their four legged friends can happily coexist."-Susan , Pembroke,MA

In the United States, there are almost 70 million dogs and 4.5 million reported dog bites a year. The majority of bites are to children ages 4-9 and 75% of bites are to a child's face by dogs belonging to the child's family. Here are some safety guidelines to help prevent a bite!

When you see a dog you don't know, STOP. Say hello to the owner and ask to say Hi from a distance.

Be a dog friend, walk slow and calm. STOP 3 feet before the dog. Wait for the dog to come over to you and stand with your hand low or to your sides. Talk gently and let the dog sniff you. This is how they get to know you.

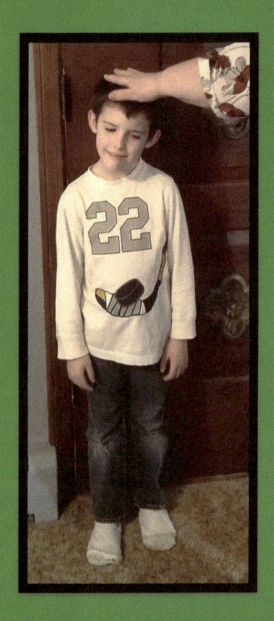#

You wouldn't like a stranger to pet you on the head would you?

Dogs don't like it either.

Be a dog Friend!

Ask the owner where the dog likes to be pet. Pet the hair so it lies smooth. After 1,2,3 take a step back and give the dog a break.

We like to look people in the eye.

Dogs don't!
Staring at a dog will make it scared and nervous.

Would **YOU** like someone touching YOUR food while you are trying to eat?

Dogs don't like it either. Give them space when they eat.

Would **YOU** like a stranger coming up to you when in your car?

Dogs don't like it either! They feel trapped and nervous and may bark or bite.

Respect a dog's personal space. When a dog is tied up or in a crate or car, it is unsafe to go to the dog

If a dog is wearing a vest or focused on its owner, never approach it. They are working and you would take them away from their important job.

If you see a loose or hurt dog, don't approach it, find an adult.
Animals who are hurt or scared may bite or chase.

If you see a strange dog, walk away quietly and gently. Don't run away, dogs love to chase things that move.

When you see a strange dog and you don't want it to bother you, stand still, arms crossed, look away to the ground. Ask an adult to help keep you safe.

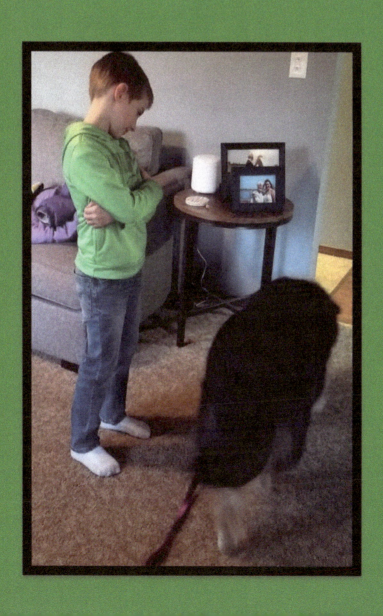

So how can we know what a dog is telling us?

Here are a few things to learn to help you be a dog friend.

Dogs are very different from us!
We use WORDS to talk.

They mostly use their BODY!

Watch their: mouth, eyes, body and tail

A yawn doesn't always mean your dog is tired. It can mean your dog is stressed and is letting you know it.

If your dog snarls, barks at you or growls, leave him be!

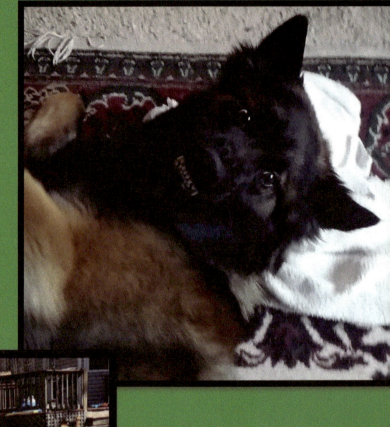

Watch for a "Whale Eye"- when the dog shows the whites of its eyes. This dog is warning you he is uncomfortable with what you are doing, so stop and give the dog space.

Dogs really don't like hugs. They feel trapped. Pet your dog for 1,2,3 instead of hugging. Be a dog friend and tell others your dog isn't a toy and isn't for hugs.

If your dog walks away, she needs space, let her be and give her a break.

A wagging tail is not always a happy tail!
If their body is wiggling, the tail is wagging and they are smiling and bright eyed, then the dog is happy.

A tail between their legs and their head down means they are uncomfortable or nervous about something, give that dog space and stay away.

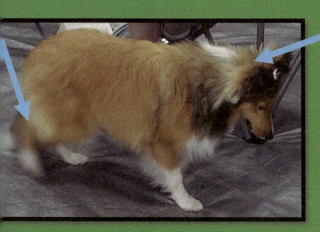
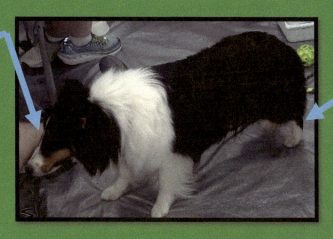

A tail that is wagging very fast, stiff and high on the body is a dog that is anxious, give that dog space and stay away.

Remember dogs are not toys or dolls, they are an animal. Treat them with respect. Don't tease them or do things that make them uncomfortable and they will be your best friend!

CPSIA information can be obtained
at www.ICGtesting.com
Printed in the USA
BVHW050037280121
598884BV00002B/17